IT COULDN'T HAPPEN, BUT IT DID

Margaret J. Anderson

HARVEST HOUSE PUBLISHERS
Irvine, California 92714

IT COULDN'T HAPPEN, BUT IT DID

Copyright © 1980 by Harvest House Publishers
Irvine, California 92714

Library of Congress Catalog Number 79-56817
ISBN 0-89081-213-6

All rights reserved. No portion of this book may be reproduced in any form without the written permission of the Publisher.

Printed in the United States of America.

Trust in the Lord with all your heart
and lean not unto your own understanding;
in all your ways acknowledge Him,
and He shall direct your paths.
—Proverbs 3:5-6

BEYOND COMPREHENSION

Lord,
I praise You
for familiar,
time-tested order—
day and night,
mind and breath,
heartbeat and sight.

I praise You, too,
for fathomless,
improbable order—
appointments, which,
meshing time
and circumstance,
appear mysteriously
out of nowhere.

We rationalize,
"They cannot happen."
Yet they do,
because You
will them to.
—Margaret J. Anderson

CONTENTS

1. In the Nick of Time 9
2. He Heard the Lord Call His Name 11
3. Calendar Legacy 13
4. For Want of a Suit 19
5. Shopping-List Prayer 23
6. An Interrupted Nap 25
7. Ming Lan, Chosen Child 27
8. Fanbelt Fanfare 31
9. I Didn't Understand 33
10. On Schedule 35
11. Toppled Plans 37
12. Seeing Is Believing 39
13. Our Extremity, God's Opportunity 41
14. Lovelift Delay 43
15. Miracles, Miracles 45
16. Red-Lined Bible 49
17. Open the Door, Lord 51
18. Quick, Lord! 53
19. About Time 55
20. No Bananas! 57
21. Hole in the Rock 59
22. A Sliver of Time 61
23. The Lost Tooth 63
24. The Elusive Magazine 65
25. Guestbook Assurance 67
26. Without Reservation 69
27. He Holds the Whole World
    in His Hands 71

28.	A Call Is Not All	75
29.	Is There a Doctor in the House	77
30.	Unscheduled Surgery	79
31.	Mother's Bible	81
32.	Rooming House Dilemma	85
33.	The Miracle Whistle	87
34.	Hunger Sated	89
35.	Verified Claims	93
36.	Impossible To Believe	95
37.	Veil of Safety	97
38.	Of Course!	99
39.	Predated Prayer Answer	101
40.	Ordered By The Lord	103
41.	Foretaste Of Heaven	105
42.	One Thing Led To Another	107
43.	A Dream And A Stolen Tractor	109
44.	Choices: Life's Building Blocks	111
45.	An Unscheduled Call	113
46.	Button, Button, Where Is My Button?	115
47.	His Dream—A Hidden Door Of Hope	117
48.	Her Torch Of Freedom	119
49.	Desert Venture	121
50.	How Could It Happen?	125

1

IN THE NICK OF TIME

I was eleven, living in an off-the-beaten-path area of northern Minnesota, when I was stricken by an illness so pain-wracking I prayed I could die.

"Just a bad stomachache" my father insisted.

Mother agreed . . . until she watched my condition worsen, then become critical.

"We must get her to a doctor. At once."

Since we didn't have a car, and our small town didn't have a doctor, Dad had to scout around for someone who could take me to one.

On Friday of that week he contacted a friend and asked him to take me to Ely, a community forty miles east of our home. There a Two Harbors' physician dispensed medical care on Sundays.

"Sorry, Charlie," Dad's friend told him. "Sunday is out . . . big family gathering at my wife's folks. How about tomorrow? There's a resident doctor in Virginia, only thirty miles away."

"Think he's any good?" Dad asked.

"A bit grouchy, but as good as doctors come."

"He'll do," Dad answered. So the men agreed on a time of departure.

That night I reached some kind of plateau. Strangely, the pain subsided temporarily. But I was still sick, miserably sick.

I felt worse on Saturday. I recall wincing repeatedly

as we drove the thirty miles on rough roads, to the hospital, where my stomachache was diagnosed as a ruptured appendix.

I was scheduled for immediate surgery. After the doctor assured me that all would be well, I relaxed and accepted the anesthetic, confident that I was in good hands.

As I hovered on the brink of ethereal unconsciousness, however, the grouch in the doctor came alive. Speaking to his nurse, he snarled, "These farmers! They bring their kids in half-dead and expect us to save them. It's a good thing this one got here today. Tomorrow would have been too late."

Despite what he said, even Saturday proved dangerous, for death kept watch at my door. Two weeks passed before the doctor pronounced me out of danger.

Looking back, I've often wondered why, of the many friends that Dad might have asked to take me to a doctor, he chose the one whose car was available, not on Sunday, but on Saturday, the day that meant life to me instead of death.

2

HE HEARD THE LORD CALL HIS NAME

John Notehelfer, oldest son of German missionary parents working in Japan, attended a Chicago seminary on a cut-every-corner, shoestring budget.

One night he awakened with a start and sat up. Surely someone had called his name. He waited. When nothing happened he lay down and tried to go back to sleep, but to no avail. He was unable to shake the feeling that someone needed him. Bewildered, he prayed, "God, who is it?"

In class the next morning fellow students began discussing a portion of Scripture that deals with the right use of money. The mysterious voice returned. "What are you going to do with that ten-dollar bill you have in your pocket?"

To John, his personal need dictated its only logical use.

At that moment a student from India walked into the room, haggard from what appeared to be lack of sleep. A strange feeling of urgency came over John. It was as if someone whispered, "Give him the money."

Mentally John scoffed. "My money? The ten dollars I need so badly?"

12/IT COULDN'T HAPPEN, BUT IT DID

But the feeling persisted.

Later, between classes, John folded the ten-dollar bill and handed it to his dark-skinned colleague.

The man looked at John warily. "Why did you do that?" he asked.

"I don't know," John answered. "I just felt compelled to."

The Indian student stared at John. When he spoke, his eyes brimmed with tears. "Last night my wife and I couldn't sleep," he said. "Out of food, we prayed that God would somehow provide money so we could buy our baby some milk."

John grinned. "And last night, I suspect at that very time, God tagged me for the job."

3
CALENDAR LEGACY*

The gatekeeper of the Shenkiu, China, mission compound approached Margaret Hillis apprehensively. Bowing low, he introduced his companion, the colonel who commanded the troops guarding the city from the approaching Japanese army.

"Heh-si-mu (pastor's wife)," the gatekeeper began, "his excellency, the colonel, has a message for you."

The colonel nodded. "The enemy is advancing into Honan Province. We have orders to evacuate the city. You must seek refuge in one of the rural villages immediately."

Margaret crossed her hands over the sleeves of her padded *e-shang* and bowed politely, thanking the man for his gracious concern. She would seriously consider his warning. As the men turned to leave, the baby began to cry. Margaret quickly closed the door on the icy January air. She hurried to comfort her child. Holding the baby close, she sighed deeply. The magnitude of her dilemma overwhelmed her.

The day before, her very sick husband, Dick Hillis, had been taken by rickshaw to a hospital 115 miles away. She and the baby, Margaret Anne (two months old), and her son (a little over a year older) were meant to await his return. She glanced at the calendar

14/IT COULDN'T HAPPEN, BUT IT DID

hanging on the wall. *January 15.* It would be sometime in February before Dick would be able to return. What would she and the two young missionary girls do if the Japanese took the city? Evacuate? How could they?

By midafternoon the army garrison had left the city. Panic erupted and a mass exodus began. One-by-one, families packed their belongings and fled.

The elders of the church pleaded with Margaret to accompany them. "We will care for you while Pastor Hillis is away."

Margaret shook her head. How could she, without offending, explain to these dear people that she couldn't take her children into homes where three and four generations crowded together amid vermin in unheated, mud-floor huts? They held death for Western babies! No, she'd have to stay where she could boil dishes, milk, and water.

Margaret bowed and thanked her friends. "I will wait here for my husband's return," she told them.

She slept poorly that night. As the wind rattled the waxed-paper window panes, she prayed for the safety of her household.

As was her custom, at breakfast the next morning she walked over to the calendar and tore off the previous day's January 15 page. The Scripture verse printed below the new date fairly leaped at her. "What time I am afraid, I will trust in Thee" (Psalm 56:3).

IT COULDN'T HAPPEN, BUT IT DID/15

By midmorning the third day the city was almost completely deserted. A servant girl had left to return to her home in the country. The boy who milked the mission goats and did the cooking quietly slipped away.

Margaret began to have misgivings about her decision to stay. It was noon before she ripped off the January 16 calendar page. She read the new message: "They that know Thy name will put their trust in Thee, for Thou, Lord, hast not forsaken them that seek Thee (Psalm 9:10).

That night Margaret pondered the message of the Scripture. How great, actually, was her faith? Could she believe that her children would be fed? She prayed repeatedly for guidance as she strove to ignore the distant gunfire that kept her awake. Perhaps she could learn to milk the goats.

For breakfast she prepared rice gruel for herself and her companions. Then she tore the page from the calendar. She gasped. "I will nourish you and your little ones" (Genesis 50:32).

It was uncanny. Curious, Margaret examined the back of the calendar pad. She learned that it had been put together in England the previous year. Yet an all-knowing God had provided the very words she needed exactly a year later!

While the missionaries were eating their gruel, a little woman, Mrs. Lee, stepped into the room carrying a pail of steaming milk. "May I stay and help you?"

16/IT COULDN'T HAPPEN, BUT IT DID

she asked. "See, I have milked the goats."

That afternoon a loud rapping at the gate brought fear to the compound. Mrs. Lee gathered enough courage to open it. She returned with a smile. "Geetze! Geedan!" she exclaimed. "Chicken! Eggs!"

The calendar promise had indeed proved true.

The next day's verse read, "When I cry unto Thee, then shall my enemies turn back: this I know, for God is for me" (Psalm 56:9). But this was a promise that Margaret had difficulty believing.

As the gunfire drew close, she and her companions prepared the house for the anticipated invasion. They hid or destroyed all papers which might be construed as having military or political significance. By nightfall the gunfire appeared to be coming from two sides of the city. Everyone retired fully dressed, prepared at any moment to rise and face the Japanese invaders.

Startled, Margaret awakened to a strange, almost eerie quietness. She heard no tramping feet, no screaming shells—only the soft murmur of little Johnny awakening in his crib.

"I will investigate," Mrs. Lee told her. She returned, shaking her head. "There is no one in the streets," she reported.

Suddenly, as they stood in the gateway, the streets began to fill—not with Japanese soldiers, but with townspeople returning from their country hiding places.

The colonel informed Margaret that the Japanese had suddenly withdrawn their troops. No, they had not been defeated. The enemy had simply turned back.

Margaret returned to the house. Her hand caressed the calendar. Calendar? More likely *a messenger from God,* she thought.

Adapted from *China Assignment,* by Dick Hillis (Overseas Crusade, Inc., Palo Alto, California).

4

FOR WANT OF A SUIT

Michigan residents Ted and Rema Van Wyke began their married life at the height of the depression, in 1933. Fortunately, Ted found work. But the job paid poorly. Furthermore, it provided little challenge and no future. Ted stuck with it, however. What else could he do?

Then in 1936 he learned of a job opening he felt would provide the incentive he needed. After applying for the position he was told that, though the branch manager was impressed with his credentials, the final decision would be made by the home-office personnel manager, with whom an interview would be arranged the next time he came to town.

Hope soared. Practical Rema approached the situation more cautiously, however. "Ted, you can't afford a new suit. What will you wear to the interview?"

"What I have on. Cleaned and pressed, it will have to do."

"I wish your brother would come through with some of those fancy discards he promised you."

Ted's brother, Bliss, the pianist for a band that at that time appeared at the Ambassador Hotel in Los Angeles, also did music adaptations for Warner

20/IT COULDN'T HAPPEN, BUT IT DID

Brothers. He had visited Ted and Rema the previous winter. Preparing for a hunting trip in the northern part of the state, Bliss had donned a pair of Ted's old trousers and a jacket that had seen better days. To his surprise, Bliss discovered that he and Ted wore the same size clothing.

"Say, would you be offended if I sent you some of my suits from time to time?" Bliss asked Ted. "You know how it is in my work—big wardrobe turnover."

"Offended? Man, anytime!" Ted had told his brother.

But now, it appeared that Bliss had forgotten his promise.

Shortly before noon a few days after Ted and Rema had spoken about the suit problem, Ted received a phone call informing him that the home-office personnel manager had arrived. Could Ted come in for a two o'clock interview?

Ted rushed hom to tell Rema the news. Hurrying to get out of the car, he dropped the briefcase. He stooped to retrieve it. Rr-rr-ip! Oh, no! He reached to investigate. His pants had split beyond repair. Now what would he do? Wear an overcoat? Call and say he was ill? Was all his hope for nothing?

Dejected, he walked up the steps to his second-floor apartment as would a robot. Rema would be heartbroken.

When he reached the top landing, someone called his name. It was the mailman. "Mr. Van Wyke, a package for you."

Ted rushed to open the box. "Man!" he exclaimed as he held up a beautifully tailored, chocolate-brown business suit.

Bliss had remembered! But, knew, *Someone Else* had done the prompting!

5

SHOPPING-LIST PRAYER

Several years ago, while the war was raging in Europe and supplies were cut off to many countries, Jennie Gailey Johnston became pregnant. In time she and her husband ran out of provisions and were forced to rely entirely on foods such as the nationals ate. That would not have been difficult if they had been nutritionally adequate. Apparently they weren't. Within a short time Jennie's strength dissipated. The slightest exertion left her exhausted.

"You need some energy-building sugar in your diet," her husband told her. She agreed. But where could they get some?

Mr. Johnston contacted Greek traders who traveled through the area and asked them to deliver some sugar and some writing paper. Because the Johnstons' supply had been depleted, they had been unable to communicate with relatives and supporting friends. The Johnstons knew that their friends wondered what had happened to them.

The traders ignored Mr. Johnston's request.

"Let's talk to God about our needs," Mr. Johnston suggested.

They did, and since they had been without light for months, Jennie added an item. "Let's ask for

24/IT COULDN'T HAPPEN, BUT IT DID

candles, too."

"We can do without them," her husband countered. "We'd better stick to essentials."

Three days after they knelt and prayed, a black messenger from Western Congo (now Zaire) arrived with a package from the Reverend C.T. Studd. He had sent it in appreciation for some kindness Mr. Johnston had shown his missionaries. Jennie tore into the package. It contained three items: two gallon cans of sugarcane syrup, three thick pads of writing paper, and two packages of candles.

Remarkable? Yes, but no more remarkable than the timing of the gift. The messenger had begun his delivery trek *the day before* the Johnstons asked God to undertake in their behalf.

"It shall come to pass that before they call, I will answer. . . ." (Isaiah 65:24).

6

AN INTERRUPTED NAP

Having completed the few household tasks she usually did while her nine-month-old daughter, Janet, napped, Darlene Potter sat down to rest.

Suddenly she felt a strange urge to get out of the house. Hurry! Scarcely thinking about her actions, she awakened Janet (a no-no under ordinary circumstances), put her into a stroller, and headed down the walk.

A block from her home she stopped, suddenly out of breath. "Slow down," she told herself. "What's your hurry?"

At that precise moment explosive booms shook the air. Darlene spun around. Were those flames she saw? Surely not the home she and Dave had come to love so well!

Panic-stricken, she began to retrace her steps. Fire engines roared by. She quickened her pace. Oh, no! A gasp escaped her lips. Tongues of flame rose from a neighbor's garage. Strange, Darlene thought; the roof's gone. Then . . . what are the firemen doing? Why are they dousing our roof?

She soon learned why. A car on which her neighbor had been working had ignited. As a result the gas tank exploded, hurling his garage roof fifty feet into the air. Aflame, it landed on top of Darlene and Dave's house, where it burned a hole through the roof. A portion dropped through the ceiling of baby Janet's bedroom.

After the fire had been extinguished, one of the firemen emerged from the house carrying a smoldering crib mattress, the one on which Janet had been napping a short time before.

7

MING LAN, CHOSEN CHILD

Ming Lan was brokenheartd when her missionary mother, Elsa Hammerlind, was forced to place her in an orphanage when she had to flee China and return to the United States.

In her loneliness, Ming Lan often recalled the story Elsa had told her about the Japanese bombing of the missionary compound in Nancheng, Hupeh Province, that led to her becoming the missionary's daughter.

It was a beautiful day. Billowing clouds drifted across the clear blue sky. Then the alert sounded and the attack began. First there was the drone of enemy planes, then the sharp repercussion of exploding bombs.

Hoping to protect her youngest children, Mrs. Chang (one of the pastor's wives) wrapped a heavy quilt around them and pulled them close. In doing so she took the full brunt of a terrific blast. An arm and a leg were severed. Soon it became apparent that she would not survive.

A week later she called Elsa to her bedside. "Sister Han," she said, "Will you take my baby, Ming Lan, as your own child and care for her and teach her to love God? My husband will have to flee. What would

28/IT COULDN'T HAPPEN, BUT IT DID

he do with a little girl only a year-and-a-half old? Please?"

Elsa looked down into the pleading eyes. What could she say? The woman's urgency was like a mighty wind in the room.

"I will, Mrs. Chang. I'll take your little girl. I'll love her and teach her to love the Lord we love."

It wasn't until Mrs. Chang had been buried that Elsa realized to what extent she had committed herself. What would she, an unmarried missionary nurse, do with a small child?

In His infinite wisdom God pointed the way. A refugee woman, a Christian convert, arrived at the compound seeking shelter. She would help in any way she could, she told the missionaries.

Elsa hired her to help care for Ming Lan.

The missionaries were permitted to work in Nan-Chang for three-and-a-half more years. During that time an inseparable bond was established between Ming Lan and her new mother, Elsa Hammerlind.

Suddenly the war stepped up its fury. The missionaries were told to evacuate immediately. The sad news: Elsa could not take Ming Lan to America even though she had obtained the father's signature for her release. The U.S. government, she learned, had overextended its Oriental quota by ten years.

After much searching she located an orphanage run by German sisters, who promised they would care for Ming Lan until she could make other arrangements.

It was a bitter parting, Ming Lan recalls. Elsa comforted her the best she could. "I'll come back as soon as I can. And remember, every day I'll pray that God will keep you safe and well. Will you pray for me?"

Sobbing, Ming Lan promised she would.

Now Mrs. Sidney-Wong (a doctor's wife in Honolulu), Ming Lan recalls two incidents when God miraculously intervened in her life.

Shortly after breakfast one morning, Ming Lan stepped through the exit that opened into the playground. At that very moment a teenage boy rushed out behind her. Roughly pushing her aside, he tore across the playground.

Instantly a scream pierced the air. Ming Lan saw the boy grab his leg as a dog disappeared through the playground gate. Investigating, the sisters learned he had been bitten by the dog. He died a painful death from rabies some days later.

"Why was I pushed aside?" Ming Lan asks. "I do not know. But I do know that, if I had been the first person on the playground that morning, I would not be alive today."

The second incident took place following a reunion with her mother in China that led to a second evacuation—this time to Hong Kong. Mother Elsa determined that she would not go back to America without her Chinese daughter.

Elsa pursued every possible avenue trying to

30/IT COULDN'T HAPPEN, BUT IT DID

secure permission to take Ming Lan to America with her. When all efforts failed, she began working with a missionary organization in Hong Kong.

"Doesn't God answer prayers?" Ming Lan wanted to know.

"Yes," Elsa told her. "But he doesn't always say *yes*. Sometimes He says *no*. At other times he says *wait*."

"Then we will wait," Ming Lan replied with confidence.

Not long this time, God decreed. At the end of the month Elsa received word that the needed permission had been granted, through a special act of Congress, initiated by a senator from Michigan, Gerald R. Ford.

8

FANBELT FANFARE

Traveling over the ridge route from Los Angeles to Grapevine, California, at the highest speed permitted, Roy Sveven suddenly noticed that his car was overheated. Dismayed, he pulled onto a safety zone and lifted the hood to investigate. A broken fanbelt! And he was miles from the nearest gas station. Now he'd never make the appointment that could lead to a coveted job.

Just then a battered Volkswagen pulled onto the safety zone behind him. Out stepped three long-haired, scruffy-looking fellows. Oh, no, Roy thought. Not them, too!

"Need some help?" the driver asked.

"Fanbelt's broken. If you fellows will stop at the next gas station and ask them to send—"

"No need," the young man interrupted. "I think I have an extra one in my car. We'll see if it fits."

"If it's for a Volkswagen. . . ."

"It isn't. Belongs to my old man."

The young man hurried to the car and dug into the trunk. "Here it is. My dad drives the same model car you do."

Roy reached for the belt. "I can—"

"I'll take it from here," the tallest, scruffiest of the

group told him. "I'm a mechanic."

When the boys had finished replacing the fanbelt Roy pulled his billfold from his pocket. The boys motioned him to forget it.

He insisted.

"No way!"

"Then, thanks. I don't know what I would have done."

"You're welcome," the owner of the car replied. "We're just servants of the good Lord. He times things just right, doesn't He?"

9

I DIDN'T UNDERSTAND

One day shortly before I was to be graduated from the teacher-training department of the University of Minnesota, my children's literature teacher detained me when class was dismissed.

She embraced me, then handed me a book. "Take this," she said. "It was written by a former student of mine. Because I have enjoyed it so much, I keep a supply on hand. Each year I present one or two copies to students I believe will profit from reading it."

I thanked the woman for the book and also for the lessons she had taught me. She had given me more than book knowledge. She had taught me patience, fortitude, and courage.

Extremely frail, she arrived at school each day in a taxi. When her classes, purposely scheduled for morning hours, were finished, she returned to her home, again in a cab. She spent afternoons in bed, correcting papers and planning the next day's classroom procedures.

I unwrapped her gift in my dormitory room. I gasped when I saw its title. "Oh, no!" I exclaimed. then, showing the book to my roommate, I asked, "Who does she think I am?"

34/IT COULDN'T HAPPEN, BUT IT DID

I put the book away and for years forgot all about it. I taught school, married, and gave birth to two lovely children. Eventually I began to write.

Then one day I came upon the book my teacher had given me. "Oh, my Lord, I didn't know . . ." I cried penitently. "but she knew."

The title of the book?

The Workmanship of Words.

10

ON SCHEDULE

Wrestling with a decision pressed upon us, my husband and I wondered which of our friends we ought to confide in. Constrained by Christ's teaching to pursue a particular course of action even though we knew it would be misunderstood, we felt we ought to talk to someone we trusted—someone who would give us impartial, reliable counsel.

Shortly before I left for Chicago to attend one of our denomination's national board meetings, my husband suggested that we contact a Christian friend, a philosophy professor who was an in-demand conference speaker.

"How?" I countered. "He teaches all week and flies to speaking engagements every weekend. Besides, think of the hundreds of miles involved."

"Let's pray about it," my husband answered. "Perhaps we'll think of someone else by the time you return."

A week later, my board meeting completed, a sister took me to O'Hare Airport, where I was to catch my return plane. Arriving early, I advised her not to park. "I'll check my bags and spend waiting time reading," I told her.

At the gate where I was to board my plane I found I

couldn't check in until another plane arrived and its passengers deplaned. "It will take approximately one-half hour," an airline attendant informed me.

I crossed the corridor, found a seat, sat down, and opened the paperback I carried with me for such emergencies. Then for some unknown reason I glanced at the man who sat next to me.

I gasped! "Dr. Bob!" I exclaimed.

Beside me sat the friend my husband and I had expressed a desire to confer with!

He told me he expected to leave from a section several gates away. A behind-schedule plane had to arrive and deplane, however, before his plane seat could be assigned. With a half-hour at his disposal, he too had decided to spend it reading.

Quickly I told him what was on my mind. After discussing the problem thoroughly, he said he concurred with our decision. Then he prayed. He thanked God for permitting us to meet. He asked that my husband and I be given courage to match our convictions.

"Don't ever think our meeting was a coincidence," he told me as we parted, he to fly east, I to fly west. "Only God can dovetail schedules so precisely."

11

TOPPLED PLANS

A few years ago, John Lindskoog, then Wycliffe Linguistics Director in Quito, Ecuador, paced the floor of his home praying that God would help him find someone to relieve the nurses at Shell Mara. At the point of collapse from long hours of work in caring for the Auca polio victims who had been flown from the medical center at Tiwaeno, they needed help immediately.

Ruth! The name of his brother's daughter flashed through his mind. Turning to his wife, he asked, "Do you know where Ruth is working now?"

"The last I knew she was at the Oakland County Hospital," his wife answered. "But don't you remember? In his last letter Wally said something about her moving to Chicago."

"I wonder how I can reach her most quickly. I know . . . through phone-patch radio. I'll get in touch with the family. They'll know where she is at this moment."

John wasted no time contacting a sister in Turlock, California. "Try to locate Ruth. Tell her we need her to relieve the nurses who are caring for the Auca polio victims. If she can, tell her to come at once. We're desperate."

38/IT COULDN'T HAPPEN, BUT IT DID

At that very moment Ruth Linkskoog was completing final arrangements to move back to Chicago, where she had accepted a nursing position at her alma mater, the Swedish Covenant Hospital. Plane reservations had been made. At any moment someone would call to pick up the trunk she had packed to send by railway express.

She looked at her watch. In less than ten minutes she'd be able to call a cab and be on her way to the airport. She was relieved, because the Chicago hospital would be a welcome change from her hectic stint at Oakland County.

The phone rang. Startled, Ruth answered it. On the other end of the line her aunt relayed John Lindskoog's message. "Are you free to go? Immediately?" she asked.

"I don't know. . . . I'm waiting for a man to pick up my trunk. He should be . . . oh, he's at the door now. I'll call you back."

Ruth walked to the door slowly. What a strange turn of events, she thought. Was it providential that her uncle's urgent request reached her at this precise moment? A few more moments of time and it would have been too late.

She stopped, closed her eyes, and whispered, "Lord, I'll go." Then she opened the door and dismissed the bewildered railroad employee with a generous tip and a mysterious, "God topped my plans."

12
SEEING IS BELIEVING

One day Fern Wickstrom, house mother for missionary students in Karawa, Zaire, discovered she couldn't read as well as she used to. This worried her. She wasn't due for a furlough for several months. Living in a remote part of the country, she was afraid of what might happen to her eyes in that interim.

When she told a doctor friend about her problem, she joshed, "I suppose I'd better call my optometrist and make an appointment to have my eyes examined."

Her doctor friend played along with her. "You don't have to do that," she said. "Come to my office. I have a whole drawer full of eyeglasses." She explained that though they were reserved for the Africans, she would make an exception for Fern.

In the doctor's office Fern did what the nationals do when their eyesight fails. She tried on pair after pair of glasses until she found one that improved her vision greatly.

"These will do," she said. Again joshing, "And how much do I owe you?"

"No charge. Just promise me you'll consult an optometrist or an oculist the moment you arrive in the United States on your next furlough."

40/IT COULDN'T HAPPEN, BUT IT DID

Fern did just that. Upon arrival in the States she consulted an optometrist as soon as she could. He tested her eyes, then carefully checked and rechecked the glasses she wore.

Suddenly he looked up from his calculations. "You know," he said, "I wouldn't suggest you change your glasses now. I believe you can wear them another term."

13

OUR EXTREMITY, GOD'S OPPORTUNITY*

Missionary Rees Howells and his wife awaited prayed-for funds to pay their train fare to London, where passage had been arranged for their journey to Gazaland, Africa. The last mail arrived without the needed funds. To further complicate matters, their train was due to leave before the mail arrived the next day.

Nevertheless, with only ten shillings to their name, Rees Howells and his wife decided to go as far as they could on that amount. They bought tickets to Llanelly, twenty miles from their home. "Our extremity will be God's opportunity," Rees Howells reasoned.

The next morning a large number of friends gathered at the depot to see them off. Some traveled as far as Llanelly with them. There, supposedly, after a brief layover the Howells would board a train for London.

When it was time to leave, Howells couldn't understand why the Lord hadn't intervened in their behalf. Then it seemed that the Spirit of God spoke to him. "What would you do if you had the money?"

"I'd take my place in the ticket line."

42/IT COULDN'T HAPPEN, BUT IT DID

"Well, what are you waiting for?"

Reese Howells stepped into the ticket line. With about a dozen persons ahead of him, he moved closer and closer to his goal. Finally there was only one man ahead of him. Then suddenly, he stood alone. "Now what, God?"

At that precise moment, a businessman stepped out of the crowd that had come to see the Howells off. He rushed over to Rees Howells. "I can't wait any longer," he told the missionary. "I must go and open my store. Here, take this." He presented thirty shillings into Howells' hand.

When the Howells arrived in London, a member of their missionary board said he held fifty pounds reserved for them. He just hadn't gotten around to mailing it.

"Thank God you didn't," Howells told him.

To himself, he said, "I wouldn't have missed that ticket-line testing for anything."

---

*Adapted from *Rees Howells: Intercessor*, by Norman P. Grubb (Lutterworth Press, 1952).

14

LOVELIFT DELAY

Tense with apprehension under the stress of the moment, World Vision Director Stanley Mooneyham prayed that the delays experienced in securing plane clearance at Bangkok would not interfere with this first LOVELIFT of orphans from Pnompenh, Cambodia.

The Convair 240, piloted by Bill Taylor, was a half-hour past the loading time permitted at the Pochentong Airport. Besides, before loading the orphans, the crew had to unload supplies for the World Vision medical team.

As Taylor banked the plane for the landing approach, a pall of black smoke from a recently bombed napalm storage dump partially obscured his vision. The wheels touched the runway. Now things had to happen speedily—a quick turnabout and a fast taxi to the apron. Then to everyone's dismay the door jammed. Panic took over until hammer blows secured its release so the ramp could be dropped.

The crew grabbed flak jackets and helmets.

Cargo was unloaded.

Spaced one hundred feet apart as a precaution against rocket attack, three vans carrying the baby orphans moved onto the field.

44/IT COULDN'T HAPPEN, BUT IT DID

Loving hands quickly transferred the woven baskets with their precious cargoes to the plane.

Then—a relayed message from World Vision's Cambodia Director, Min Tien Voan. At the airport with his wife and small children he needed one more emigration stamp, for his wife's passport.

Time had run out.

Voan urged the plane to leave. "You'll jeopardize the lives of the orphans. We'll come some other time."

Sick at heart, Mooneyham agreed to leave the family.

Ramp up.

Door secure.

Start the engine.

The prop turned sluggishly. Engine failed to cooperate.

Again! Groan. . . .

Three minutes . . . four . . .

Suddenly, waving his precious document, Min Tien Voan alerted the plane. In a moment he and his wife and children were hurried aboard. He had secured the final stamp needed for his wife's departure.

The engine revved and caught. Elapsed time from touchdown to takeoff: fifty minutes. Praise God!

Silently Mooneyham addressed his Maker: "Even delays are part of Your timing."

15

MIRACLES, MIRACLES

"How about a walk through the redwoods?" a close friend, Jeanette Sporrong, asked me one day at a West Coast women's retreat. "I have a burden I'd like to discuss with you."

In the cool, hushed quietness of the giant trees she told me that she and her husband were deeply concerned about their daughter's and their son-in-law's welfare. In England, studying and seeking meaning for their lives, they had purchased and renovated an old sea-faring vessel that they used for living quarters and traveling jaunts.

After being shipwrecked in an English-channel storm, they barely escaped with their lives. Having lost all their personal belongings, they sold as junk (on a promise-to-pay-as-you-can agreement) materials salvaged from the boat when it was washed ashore.

"I wish they would visit L'Abri (Francis Schaeffer's Switzerland Christian training center)," Jeanette told me. "I believe they might find the direction they are seeking. I'm going to write Ruth and suggest that she and Steve try to get in. Will you join me in praying for them?"

"You know I will," I answered. "How about now?"

We stopped in a spot where sunlight filtered through the massive redwoods, momentarily wrapping us in its warmth and God's holy presence. Simply, honestly, we made our requests known to God.

Before writing her letter, however, Jeanette airmailed a Bible to Ruth to replace the one lost at sea. Then, as concerned about the young people as Jeanette, and unknown to her, Steve's mother airmailed a copy of Mrs. Schaeffer's book *L'Abri* to them.

By now the young people had set up housekeeping in a tent in one of Amsterdam's camping areas. One day Steve gave his last seventy cents to a Canadian lad who was hungry. Though Ruth understood this typically compassionate gesture, she worried about their own status—a broken-down car and no money with which to have it repaired so Steve could look for work.

While they were discussing their dilemma, a couple who camped nearby came to tell them they were leaving to return to the United States. "How would you like to have our bicycles?" they asked.

"Great!" Steve exclaimed. Then suddenly grave, he added, "But we have no money."

"We didn't ask you if you would like to buy the bicycles. We want to give them to you."

Steve, an able carpenter, immediately set out on his gift bike to look for work. Shortly he was halted by someone calling his name. He pulled to the curb. Running toward him was the man from France who had bought his shipwrecked boat.

"I've been looking everywhere for you. I came to pay you the rest of the money I owe."

Steve shook his head unbelievingly. "But how . . .?"

"Someone told me you might be camping here."

Within a few hours Steve had located a job, and Ruth had leased a reasonably priced apartment (almost an impossibility in those days of foreign youth influx to the city).

Then to their amazement, the Bible and the book *L'Abri,* sent by their respective mothers, arrived in the same general-delivery mail.

Of this latter experience Ruth says, "My hands shook so much I could scarcely unwrap the books. The Bible? How I had missed mine. *L'Abri?* Steve and I had talked about visiting the Schaeffers someday.

"Though I was aware the center had a long waiting list of applicants, I had mentally begun an application of my own. But now I put these thoughts aside and began to read, first from the Bible and then from *L'Abri.* Alternately laughing and crying, I realized that the same wonderful God who undertook for the Schaeffers could undertake in our lives, too. I knew I could trust him to get us to L'Abri. Look what he had already done for us."

16

RED-LINED BIBLE

It was April, shortly before Easter, when Bo, the lively middle child in the Robert Redding McConnel home, picked up his mother's Bible. Having watched her underline specific passages of Scripture, he decided he would do as she had done. He found a bright red marking pen, and, with quick and decisive (though somewhat irregular) strokes, he underlined several passages on a page he chose at random.

His father, believing that a two-and-a-half-year-old child should know better, spanked him soundly.

The next afternoon his mother, Carole McConnel, took her three children, Elizabeth, Sarah and Bo, with her to deliver an Easter lily to a friend. Without any warning, disaster struck. The car went out of control and, despite anything Carole tried to do, rammed into a metal utility pole. She and the girls suffered no injury, but Bo, who had unfastened his seat belt without his mother's knowledge, was hurled against the car's dashboard and fatally injured.

The night before the funeral Bob and Carole sat in their living room trying to comfort each other. They recalled precious moments they had enjoyed with Bo.

Suddenly remembering the spanking incident and the misdemeanor that had instigated it, Carole said,

50/IT COULDN'T HAPPEN, BUT IT DID

"Bob, let's check the Bible to see what passages he underlined."

It took some time. Finally they found the page with the red scribbling. It couldn't be. But it was! Psalm 26:6,8: "I will wash my hands in innocency. . . . Lord, I have loved the habitation of Thy house, and the place where Thy honor dwelleth. . . ."

Carole grabbed Bob's arm. "Oh, Bob, he's there now."

"Read that." Bob pointed to another verse. "The Lord is the Light of my salvation; whom shall I fear?"

"No one," Bob whispered. "No one."

17

OPEN THE DOOR, LORD

Jobs were depression-scarce in the fall of 1929, especially part-time jobs—the type that meant room and board, books and college tuition for me.

Working as a waitress in a northern Minnesota coffee shop, I had been aware of that fact all summer. I also knew that college was a closed book for me unless I obtained part-time, after-school-hours-work.

I had investigated every possibility. Nothing! "Why doesn't God answer my prayer?" I asked a friend one day.

"How much faith do you have?"

"Not much," I had to admit.

My friend rose and walked to the front door of her home. "Let me show you something," she said. "Step outside. Then walk past that second house. After I've closed the door come back and knock on it."

Puzzled, I did what she told me to. The moment I knocked the door swung open.

"Note," she said. "I opened the door the moment it was necessary. Not when you were halfway down the block. Understand?"

I wasn't sure. "You mean I must wait still longer. But school opens on Tuesday, the day after Labor

Day. What if . . .?"

My friend put her arm around my shoulder. Then she prayed. "Lord, You know exactly when Margaret needs to walk through a job door. Please open it in her moment of need."

The Wednesday before the week school opened came and went. Another day. No job. Friday I followed a fresh lead. No luck. "Sorry, I'll have to give the job to a man."

Saturday I worked the day shift at the coffee shop. That afternoon one of the waitresses called to ask if I would take her evening shift. I consented.

That evening I chanced to hear the woman with whom I worked mention to a customer friend that her husband's employer was looking for a part-time bookkeeper.

My pulse quickened. Good thing I had taken that bookkeeping course in high school, I thought!

"Think he'd consider me?" I asked. "I have to find work or I can't go on to school."

"Who knows?" the woman answered. "Why don't you contact him? He's out of town this weekend, however. Be back late Monday. You could call him at his home."

She gave me his name and address.

Was this an answer to prayer? I wondered. Did God have his hand on the doorknob?

He did. Late Monday afternoon He turned the knob. The door swung open. My schooling was assured.

18

QUICK, LORD!

It was early fall when the road-building crew moved across the road from the Derwin Myhr country home. Result: seven-day weeks of noise, dirt, sand, and limestone dust that stretched family nerves to a snapping point. When some of the men began parking their automobiles on the Myhr's tree-shaded front lawn, Derwin, a schoolteacher and a school-bus driver, exploded.

"I've had it," he stormed. "The minute I finish my route this morning I'm going to call our lawyer. This has got to stop."

Betty Myhr, his wife, tried unsuccessfully to dissuade him. The moment he left for work she began to pray. "Lord, calm him down." Suddenly realizing how often bad tempers result in accidents, her concern turned to the safety of the children that Derwin would be transporting to school that morning. She added an urgent prayer postscript: "Quick!"

A half-hour later a knock sounded at the back door. Opening it, Betty, faced three broad-shouldered men who introduced themselves as contractor and foremen in charge of the road construction.

"We came to ask if it would be all right if we paved your circular driveway."

"I. . . ." She didn't know what to say. The pocked,

gravel driveway surely needed paving. But why? Surely Derwin hadn't had time. . . .

"Strange thing," the contractor began; "We were right in the middle of today's work plans when Tom here said we ought to do something for you folks, putting up with our noise and all."

Bewildered, Betty said that she and her husband would be grateful for such kindness.

When the men left, she panicked. She had to stop Derwin. She had to stop Derwin. She phoned the school. "Will you ask my husband to call home immediately when he gets in from his bus route?"

A few minutes later the phone rang.

"Honey, you mustn't . . ." Betty began.

"Hold it," Derwin interrupted. "I know what you're going to say. But don't worry. I'm okay now. God calmed me down."

Nodding, Betty replaced the receiver slowly. Yes, she thought, who could it be but God?

19

ABOUT TIME

Shortly after my book *It's Your Business, Teenager* was published, the Braille Circulating Library, Richmond, Virginia, printed it in Braille.

My complimentary copy arrived at the time I was working on an article about a very talented teenager, Linda Boreen. She had been blinded at birth due to an overdose of oxygen, a procedure which is no longer routine, since doctors have learned that too much oxygen damages the delicate tissues of newborn infants.

I loaned the book to Linda, who circulated it among students at the School of the Blind that she attended in Faribault, Minnesota.

Several years later my daughter wrote me from Ohio, telling of a blind friend's interest in Christianity. "Mom," she asked, "will you send me your Braille book so she can read it?"

Where was it? Had Linda returned it? I didn't think so, but I wasn't sure.

Because my husband was scheduled to speak at a church we had once served (and that Linda's parents attended), I decided to wait until I talked to them before inquiring about the book.

In dismissing the Sunday morning service, the resident pastor asked me to accompany my husband to the door so we could greet our many friends as they left the church.

The church emptied slowly as individuals updated us about themselves and their families.

Then, suddenly, there stood Linda.

"Linda," I exlaimed as I embraced her.

She introduced us to her husband (we hadn't known she had married). Then she handed me the Braille copy of my book *It's Your Business, Teenager.*

"When I heard you were going to be here I realized I had never returned the book. It's about time, isn't it?" she said.

About time? I smiled. She had no way of knowing how wisely she spoke.

20

NO BANANAS!

Carol Chihocky finds that God constantly leads her into startling byways in her walk of wonder. Living on a modest medical retirement check, she has learned to make do or do without.

One day, en route to a large supermarket, her children begged her to buy some bananas.

"Not today," she told them. "Today we buy only essentials."

The children pouted. Repenting, Carol said, "Okay, let's put it this way. If God wants us to have bananas He'll arrange so we can buy them."

On entering the store the children dashed to the fruit displays. Dismayed, they exclaimed, "Wouldn't you know it—"Bananas: 27 cents a pound."

Later Carol discovered a large bag of well-ripened bananas on a ledge in the back of a store. She begun to examine them.

"Want those?" a voice asked. Carol turned. Beside her stood the store manager. "You can have the whole works for fifteen cents."

"Sold!"

When he left, Carol hurried to a scale to weigh the fruit. It came to twenty pounds—less than a penny a pound! At home the family made a more startling discovery. Not a single banana had a blemish inside!

21

HOLE IN THE ROCK

One day Edwin and Laura Solie, with their two children and a visiting friend, Beatrice, drove to Santa Cruz for a beach picnic at a spot they called "Hole in the Rock."

Because the tide was out, they strolled along the beach picking up shells and watching crabs burrow in the sand. They walked over and across slippery rocks covered with starfish, sea anemones, and barnacles. The rocks were pitted with small, water-filled potholes. The children pried starfish from the rocks and watched as the sea anemones wrapped themselves around sticks poked into their mouths.

Not until the sun began its descent in the western sky did they pack their belongings and head for their car. When Edwin reached into his pocket for the car keys, he discovered he didn't have them.

No amount of searching brought them to light. The group retraced their steps along the beach. What an impossible task, they thought. Someone could have picked up the keys or else trampled them into the sand. Nevertheless, they searched and searched. To no avail.

Finally Edwin said, "It's no use. I suppose the only thing we can do is call a garage for help." He hesitated. "No, let's pray first." His prayer was simple and direct. "Dear Lord, you know where those keys are. Please lead us to them."

Together they began what seemed a useless second search. Suddenly Beatrice shouted, "Here they are!"

Everyone breathed a sigh of relief. No one had picked up the keys. No one had trampled them into the sand. They hadn't fallen into a water-filled pothole. They lay in plain view on the spot to which God had directed the searchers!

22

A SLIVER OF TIME

As a teenager I attended a consolidated school which bussed students from near and far. The school was situated at the edge of a small northern Minnesota town. Usually those of us who rode the busses spent our noon hours in town on some personal or parental errand.

One noon as I prepared to leave with two of my friends, my homeroom teacher detained me. She asked me to help her with some task. I don't recall what it was.

"Run along," I told my friends. "I'll meet you at the post office."

I finished the task quickly and hurried to join my friends. I had gone only a short distance when I noticed a crowd of people at the railroad crossing nearby. I quickened my pace.

Something awful must have happened!

23

THE LOST TOOTH

"Oh, no, not again!" my husband exclaimed one morning as he showed me a gold-crowned tooth that had broken away from his partial denture. "This time I'm going to find someone who knows how to make it stay in place."

He phoned a dental lab for an appointment.

"Now where should I put this prize until I need it?" he asked.

"Seal it in an envelope and put it on the desk in the den," I answered.

Shortly after dinner the night before the lab appointment, a very distraught husband called to me from the den. "I can't find my tooth. I've turned this place upside down. Have you seen it?"

I assured him I hadn't and began to help him search—first in the den, then through the rest of the house. At midnight I gave up. "Let's go to bed," I suggested. "God knows where the tooth is. He can direct us to it while we sleep."

The next morning I awakened with a start. I knew! I grabbed my robe and made a dash for the utility room and the pull-out trash bin into which we emptied wastepaper for once-a-week disposal.

On entering the room I collided with my husband

heading for the same bin. There buried in a pile of wastepape lay the "tooth" envelope!

24

THE ELUSIVE MAGAZINE

In preparing to write an article about the husband-and-wife team who became Christians while photographing and researching the *Look* magazine article about the Jesus people, I knew I needed to read the article again before I interviewed them.

But I had to locate the issue that carried the story before I could read it. No simple matter, I soon discovered. It was as if the earth had opened and swallowed it.

I had loaned by copy to a friend, who couldn't remember what she had done with it. Readers had snatched the issue from magazine racks the moment it was placed for sale. I checked our local library. Someone had ripped out the specific pages I needed. Friends? They'd read the article, but they'd sent it to a son, daughter, or parent. Or, as I, they had loaned it to someone who failed to return it.

Dismayed, I began a previously scheduled automobile trip to Chicago with my husband. Surely someone there would know where I could find the magazine. "God, help me locate it," I prayed.

We neared Chicago late Wednesday afternoon. Since we weren't due in the city until Thursday noon, we decided to spend the night in one of the small towns nearby. As dusk dropped its gray veil on the

66/IT COULDN'T HAPPEN, BUT IT DID

lush green Illinois farmland, we pulled off the freeway and drove to a town a mile away.

We rejected as unsatisfactory the first motel we passed. We also rejected the next two. Since there were no others, we returned to the first one we had seen. It appeared quite satisfactory now!

My husband fell asleep soon after we retired. A habitual reader-in-bed, I reached for one of several magazines in the bottom shelf of my bedside table.

Incredible! In my hand lay the elusive *Look* magazine!

25

GUESTBOOK ASSURANCE

Enroute from Duluth, Minnesota, to a new parish in Los Angeles shortly after World War Two, my clergyman husband and I stopped to visit some friends in Nebraska. At a social gathering in our honor we spoke to a couple, Mr. and Mrs. Art Swanson, whose sun had lost his life in the South Pacific. We told them how sorrowful we had felt when we received the news of his untimely death.

"I'd feel relieved," Mrs. Swanson told us, "if we could be sure he had returned to the faith in God he once professed."

My husband took her hands in his. With all the tenderness he could muster, he said, "How do you know he didn't? Remember, the Bible says, 'Train up a child. . . .' There could have been any number of circumstances, any number of contacts, that caused him to reaffirm his commitment to God."

"Oh, I hope so. But I wish I knew."

Shortly after settling in our new parish we spent an evening with a large group of young people gathered in their youth counselor's home for an evening singspiration.

At one point, "Coach," as the young people affectionately called our host, asked those present to sign the guestbook. My husband and I purposely signed our names last. We'd done this before, knowing that by checking listed names with the route in which the book traveled, we could more quickly match names and faces.

Before I laid the book aside, however, I paged back, noting the large number of young men's names listed in a particular section. It soon became apparent from the boys' comments that they had been guests in Coach and Florence Johnson's home on their way to Pacific Navy and Army assignments.

Bob Swanson! The signature leaped from the page.

Pointing to the name, I handed the book to my husband. "Look!" I exclaimed.

"Find someone you know?" Coach asked.

"We aren't sure," I answered. "Was this Bob Swanson from Mead, Nebraska?"

"Yup!" Coach answered, his face aglow. "A fine young man. And do you know what? He reaffirmed his faith in Jesus Christ right here in this living room."

I squeezed my husband's hand. "We'll write his mother," I whispered, adding, "Isn't God good?"

26

WITHOUT RESERVATION

While vacationing in Phoenix one winter, my husband and I decided to make a weekend trip to Los Angeles via San Diego and Disneyland. As we chatted about people we would visit en route, we recalled that friends from my childhood home, two sisters and their husbands, owned a motel somewhere in California.

"It would be fun to drop in on them," I said.

"Without an address?" my husband chided. "I'm sure there are at least a hundred thousand motels in California, perhaps more. It would be as bad as hunting for a needle in ten haystacks."

After visiting with friends in San Diego, we headed north, hoping to spend the night close to Disneyland so we could visit the tourist attraction the next day. At a leisurely pace we drove along the coastal route. We didn't want to miss Laguna Beach with its art displays, as well as other places we remembered from former visits.

As we neared Disneyland we began to look for motel vacancy signs.

"Here?" my husband asked at one point.

"Not yet. Let's drive closer."

"A little later, "Here?"

I shook my head.

He drove past the motel he had inquired about, and then, after checking to see that there were no cars behind us, backed up and drove up to the motel office.

"How come?" I asked.

"I don't know. I just felt we ought to stay here." I stayed in the car while my husband went into the office to get someone to show us a room. To my amazement, out of the office stepped one of the sisters who, together with their husbands, "owned a motel somewhere in California."

"Margaret!" she exclaimed, as surprised to see me as I was to see her.

I doubt that we've ever enjoyed an evening in a motel as much as we did that one, with wonderful accommodations and meaningful, reminiscent fellowship. It was truly a reservation prearranged by God!

27

HE HOLDS THE WHOLE WORLD IN HIS HANDS

Some years ago two Sudan Inland Mission pilots, Clarence Soderberg (nicknamed Soddy) and Dick Vossler, prepared to leave Jos, Nigeria, in two separate planes. Dawn broke as they made their way to the airport.

Suddenly Dick gasped. Pointing to the sky he exclaimed, "Look!"

Soddy whistled. He knew that the solid black wall that darkened the northeastern sky could be interpreted only as a line squall, a collection of several thunderstorms. Sometimes two hundred miles long, forty thousand feet high, and a hundred miles deep, they reminded Soddy of the lyrics of a familiar song: "So high you can't get above it; so low you can't get under it; so wide you can't get around it."

Both he and Dick knew that meteorologists estimate wind speeds of two to three hundred miles an hour at the squall's vortex, and that in this vortex hailstones collect, some as large as a grapefruit.

Since both men were headed away from the storm, they knew they had to maneuver a speedy takeoff. Once aloft, they'd be safe, for these squalls were known not to deviate in their northeast-to-southwest course.

Dick, flying northwest, would miss the storm and

return that same afternoon. Soddy, flying southwest ahead of the storm, decided to spend the night at his destination, a missionary base some two hundred fifty miles from Jos.

When he landed, Soddy secured his plane and headed for the base. A nurse came running to meet him.

She greeted Soddy breathlessy. "Hurry. You must take a look at Ray Marler. He's terribly sick. I think you'll have to fly him to Jos."

"No way," Soddy answered. "I've just tied the plane down. A line squall is headed in this direction. Should be here by 3:30 this afternoon. I just beat it off the runway."

"But you have to do something," she countered. "Ray's been sick for two weeks. He's retched for four days. I don't think he can last much longer."

When Soddy saw Ray he knew he'd have to try something. The missionary had lost an immense amount of weight. Besides, he was delirious. "Get him ready," Soddy told the nurse. "I'll make preparations for a takeoff."

While he readied the plane he prayed, "Lord, here's one of your servants close to death. He needs a doctor. Lord, you made the clouds. You made the storm. You made the lightning. If you can do all these things it's a small accomplishment for you to turn this storm around so we can get through to the hospital."

IT COULDN'T HAPPEN, BUT IT DID/73

Ray was brought to the plane on a special stretcher. Once on board, the nurse, with her hypodermic equipment, sat next to him. Mrs. Marler and her baby sat in front with Soddy.

They flew for an hour. By that time they should have seen the storm. They couldn't find a trace of it, however. Another half-hour, still no sign. Another.... Suddenly, twenty minutes ahead of them, the sunlit pan of the hospital roof blinked up at them. They landed in clear sunshine. God *had done* something with that storm!

As Soddy refueled his plane, Dick Vossler flew in from the northwest. He gasped when he saw Soddy.

"What are you doing here?" he asked.

Soddy told him.

"That explains it," he said. "The line squall tagged me every inch of the way. Ever heard of one changing its course? Well, this one did. I thought I was having a nightmare. Coming back I had to fly along the northern edge of it. That's why I'm so late."

"And that's why I'm early," Soddy answered. "What say we thank God for His goodness?"

28

A CALL IS NOT ALL

In his youth Ralph Fondell and his sister listened to a missionary's come-and-help-us plea. She responded, but he did not. I'll serve Christ at home, Ralph reasoned.

However, he changed his mind while serving in the U.S. Navy. His call came in an overseas youth rally where he heard radiant testimonies by Chinese and Garumanian young people, many of whom had been won to Christ through Christian radio.

Suddenly Ralph felt a great compulsion to serve God in radio, the communication field in which he was active in the Navy. Revelation 3:8 became his directive: "I know your works [your engineering skills]; behold, I have set before you an open door."

Yet after marriage, a college degree, and further studies in radio, the door to radio service failed to open. Wisely Ralph's denomination director of world missions counseled, "Stay with radio if you feel this is where God wants you. Study and get all the practical experience you can. Who knows, we may have a place for you when you are ready."

His advice was taken reluctantly. Ralph knew that his denomination had no immediate radio plans, and he wanted to get started at once.

76/IT COULDN'T HAPPEN, BUT IT DID

While waiting for something to materialize, Ralph and his wife spent a summer in mountain mission work in Tennessee. It was there that their door of service opened a crack. Ralph was offered a job with a Christian radio station. He was delighted, for now he would obtain practical radio experience. Later he spent four years as chief engineer for another station, this time in West Virginia. The door opening widened. Yet Ralph had misgivings. Was this what God intended for him?

Apparently not. God's plan included work at still another station. There Ralph obtained valuable programming experience. Then, just when he felt he'd have to give up his dream, the door swung wide open. His denomination announced that it was ready to erect a radio station in Nome, Alaska. Where could they find an engineer with sufficient training and experience?

They turned to Ralph. He had waited ten years! At times he had felt they were endless. Looking back, he realized they were all in God's perfect timing. He wouldn't have been ready before. Now, with the maturity that comes only through experience, Ralph was able to step, adequately prepared, into the service to which God had called him.

29

IS THERE A DOCTOR IN THE HOUSE?

During the construction of a new house for the Bible Institute of Ugangi in Zaire, Ann Berg and missionary colleagues lived in a makeshift dwelling a short distance from the site of the new house.

Study was not interrupted, however. Classes met during the morning hours. After a quick lunch, the nationals, including twenty Bible institute freshmen under the supervision of missionary Dan Erickson, went to work on the main buildings and the mud-and-straw student homes. They worked hard and long, often well into the moonlit evenings.

One day Dan, who had a history of ulcers, collapsed on the dirt floor of the classroom. Somehow he managed to tell the workmen to go home and pray for him. Then he dragged himself to the missionary living quarters.

Ann panicked when she saw him. What could they do—two bumpy truck hours from a missionary doctor? And even if they could travel they would accomplish nothing. Presently the doctor was away from his home.

As she worked to make Dan as comfortable as possible, she prayed, "Lord, You are the only one who can intervene. Please help us."

God answered. It was as if He had said, "All will be well." Ann relaxed.

In the middle of the afternoon she heard a truck turn into the driveway. She rushed to investigate.

"Dr. Warren!" she shouted, overcome by joy.

"Hi, Ann," he greeted. "Just thought I'd stop by to see if everything is okay before I head for home."

With eyes wet with tears Ann answered, "It will be now." Then, lifting her face heavenward, she whispered. "Thank you, Lord."

30

UNSCHEDULED SURGERY

Henry Strube served Jesus Christ as a missionary in Columbia, South America, during the height of "evangelical persecutions." Often threatened, beaten, even arrested, he repeatedly experienced God's protection.

One day, unknown to Mr. Strube, some men were incited to kill him. Aware that he would be driving over a mountain road at a particular time, they devised a murder plan they believed could not fail.

They drove to the proposed site, then backed their truck into the side of the mountain, hidden from view beyond a treacherous curve that Mr. Strube would have to navigate. As he rounded the curve they planned to strike his vehicle broadside, sending it plummeting down the mountainside.

But as Mr. Strube and his two companions neared the area, the muffler on their car broke, creating so much noise that his enemies miscalculated their timing. As Mr. Strube rounded the curve, the men's momentary delay gave him time to swing his car sharply to the right. Thrown off balance, he grabbed the open car door for support.

He felt devastating pain in his hand as the truck sideswiped his car, turned, and sped down the mountain.

80/IT COULDN'T HAPPEN, BUT IT DID

Though Mr. Strube's life had been spared, his hand was badly mangled, two of his fingers almost completely severed.

"We must get help," he told his companions, handing one of them the keys to the car.

Together they descended the mountain as rapidly as possible.

As they neared the bottom, Mr. Strube begged them to stop. Miles from medical assistance, this ordinarily optimistic man felt he was doomed.

Just then a jeep carrying four men arrived on the scene. A tall, impressive-looking man strode toward them. He took one look at Strube's hand and said, "Those fingers must be amputated at once. Want me to do it?"

Strube grimaced, assuming he was joking.

He wasn't. A famous Edinburgh surgeon in South America on a safari, he carried a supply of medical equipment with him.

He placed a sheet on the ground, administered chloroform, then proceeded to amputate Mr. Strube's mangled fingers.

We might say, "It couldn't happen." But it did. Missionary Strube's three-fingered left hand is ample proof that it did.

31

MOTHER'S BIBLE*

When Jean D. Brewer was a child in a small Scottish village, a postman delivered a package to her father from America. It contained a pigskin-leather Bible. The inscription on the flyleaf read: To William Ingram, Sr., from his son, William Ingram, Jr."

Because Jean's father preferred using his own well-worn Bible, this gift copy became known as "Mother's Bible," for it was she who used it most frequently.

Mrs. Ingram died on Christmas Day when Jean was fourteen years old. A few days later, when Jean left Scotland to go to England, her father gave her Mother's Bible. She used it faithfully until after she married, when her husband gave her a new Bible. Fifteen years later, when she, her husband, and their three sons moved to the United States, Jean took Mother's Bible with her.

One day several months after their arrival, Jean's sister Margaret, director of a children's home, asked, "Jean, do you ever use Mother's Bible? If you aren't using it, may I have it?"

Jean knew why Margaret asked that question. When she counseled the parents of the children for whom she cared, she often ended up giving them a Bible. No doubt she had exhausted her supply.

82/IT COULDN'T HAPPEN, BUT IT DID

Jean told her sister she could use the Bible.

Several months later Margaret phoned Jean. "Jean," she said, "I have a father in my office who has come to pick up his child. I want to give him a Bible. Since they are leaving the city immediately there isn't time to buy one for him. Would you mind if I gave him Mother's Bible?"

Jean couldn't imagine a stranger using Mother's Bible, yet she felt compelled to say, "Do what you think the Lord wants you to do."

Several years passed. At the close of the morning service in a Los Angeles Christian Brethren service an elder detained Jean. "There's a man asking for someone by the name of William Ingram. Will you find out what he wants?"

As Jean walked with the elder to the back of the room, a stranger approached her. Her eyes riveted on the book he carried. Excitedly she exclaimed, "It's Mother's Bible!"

"Then my search is ended," the man told Jean. He related how one day when he passed a trashcan containing a pile of books he noticed that one was a Bible. He picked it up.

The Ingram name on the flyleaf meant nothing to him. But when he turned to the back he discovered some sermon notes and quotes from a preacher who lived in Los Angeles. Since he was going to be visiting the city, he decided to take the Bible with him. The night before, he had scanned the newspapers for the name of this preacher. He found it, and the church he served.

"So I took a chance. I decided to attend your service to see if anyone knew the owner of the Bible."

Overcome by gratitude, Jean accepted her Mother's Bible. Since that particular church rarely placed advertisements in the newspapers, she realized how precisely God had timed the ad that her benefactor had read.

Adapted from "Mother's Durable Bible," by Jean D. Brewer, in *The Christian Reader*. Used by permission of author.

32

ROOMING HOUSE DILEMMA

When Russ Chandler arrived in Edinburgh in 1955 to begin seminary studies, he went directly to a home recommended to him by a former student.

The stocky woman who greeted him at the door shook her head. "I'm sorry, you have been misinformed. Im not taking boarders anymore." Disheartened because he had made no allowance for an alternate solution to his housing problem, Russ wondered what to do.

Perhaps the American Express office could provide some information.

"Lord, undertake for me," he prayed as he approached the woman at the front desk.

"Do you know anyone who is looking for American live-in students?"

She shook her head. "No," she said, "I'm sorry. . . ."

Her telephone rang.

The woman greeted her caller, then as she listened her face brightened. She looked at Russ and shaped an okay sign with her fingers. "You are an answer to one man's prayer," she told her caller. There's a fine young man standing beside me right now who needs

...COULDN'T HAPPEN, BUT IT DID

such a home. I'll send him right over."

She hung up and repeated the question which the woman, a Mrs. Thompson, had asked her: *"Do you happen to know any American student who is looking for a place to stay during the coming school year?"*

Today when Russ Chandler recalls the experience he says, "In God's providence, she did *happen* to know such a person. I filled his shoes."

33

THE MIRACLE WHISTLE

Doe Peters of Hinsdale, Illinois, retired early that warm summer day. She fluffed her pillows and proceeded to do some leisurely reading.

Suddenly a feeling of urgent concern for her son, Bill, a commercial abalone fisherman, engulfed her. Was he in danger? she wondered. That couldn't be. Though his work required that he dive to depths of one hundred feet or more, he had always assured her that he never took chances that would endanger his life.

Pray! a voice seemed to say.

Mrs. Peters prayed: "God, you know what's happening to Bill right now. Whatever his problem, be with him; protect him."

Three hours later a telephone call awakened her. Her son was on the other end of the line. The moment he said, "Hi, Mom," she knew something unusual had happened.

"Did you pray for me a few hours ago?"

"I surely did, but how did you know?"

Bill related this tale.

"Today while diving for abalone, at a depth of seventy feet, I heard a screeching whistle. It was unlike any sound of the sea I had ever heard—sort of life a traffic cop sounding a warning signal.

"Instantly I looked around. I couldn't believe my eyes. I'd been as watchful as ever, yet here were two sharks charging toward me. A moment's hesitation would have meant sure death for me. Quickly I cut the mesh bag that I carry at my waist for gathering abalone. Then, swinging my defense bar, I began to pray. I still can't believe I surfaced safely. It was a miracle, Mom. I knew right away you must have been praying for me."

"And," his mother added, "that God heard my prayer."

34

HUNGER SATED

Pursing a Bible college education, newly married Barry and Christine Jones arrived in Toronto, Canada, from England with enough money (they thought) to last them a month. They'd been promised part-time work that would provide for their needs during the rest of the school year.

In the middle of that first month, two weeks from payday, their money was gone. Christine suspected they had enough left for two more meals. What would they do then? Pray? If Hudson Taylor and others could live by faith, couldn't they? But she and Barry weren't Hudson Taylors. They were just insignificant Bible students. Suddenly she felt like a child who, afraid of the elevators, countered her father's assurance that it really worked with these words: "I know it will, but I'm still afraid it won't."

After their meager breakfast a fellow student called to pick them up for church. "I'll be right with you," Christine told her husband, "After I get my gloves."

As she opened the dresser drawer, she spied two shiny dimes she had laid aside to send to a young nephew in England for his coin collection. *Well,* she thought, *at least we'll have a token offering.*

At the close of the service one of the elderly couples asked Barry and Chris to join them for a chicken dinner. During the meal they invited them to attend an afternoon missionary prayer service. Barry and Christine enjoyed the warm fellowship of the group, as well as the light supper that followed.

They sat with their new friends during the evening meeting. Christine wondered what they would think when she and Barry ignored the offering plate. They'd already given their last dimes. Sitting close to the aisle, their friends dropped their money into the offering plate, but instead of passing it to Barry and Christine, they handed it back to the usher. How did they know they were penniless?

The next morning, after eating the last of their bread and bacon, they set off for school. Christine's elevator faith dropped to a new low during the two-mile walk in soaring temperature. Dismally she pondered a lunchless day, then a long walk to work and home after classes had been dismissed. Midmorning they checked their mail. Nothing!

Later, as they prepared to go their separate ways to work, a classmate stopped them. "How are you doing?" he asked.

"Just fine. . . ." Barry stammered.

"Take this anyway." The young man handed Barry a crisp ten-dollar bill. "The Lord told me to give this to you."

Greatly moved, Barry and Christine expressed their gratitude. Ten dollars seemed a lot of money at the time. It paid for several lunches, bus tickets, and groceries, but it didn't last the full two weeks until payday.

Their friend came to their aid again, with an armload of groceries. This time he insisted they tell him about their financial needs. When he heard their plight he gave them what he felt would last them the rest of the month.

"We'll pay you back."

Their benefactor shook his head. "Don't repay me," he said. "But when you are able, just do unto others what I, prompted by God, have done for you."

35

VERIFIED CLAIMS

My husband and I were considering buying what appeared to be a very good used car. Though we had met the dealer on several occasions, we couldn't vouch for his integrity. We needed proof that his claims for the car were valid.

Urged to wrap up the deal, my husband hedged. "Will you let us think about it for a day or two?"

The dealer agreed to hold the car until we reached a decision.

The next day my husband was introduced to a man from a nearby town by a mutual friend. Almost immediately the conversation turned to automobiles. The man my husband had just met spoke of a car deal he had just completed.

"Not because I wanted to," the man explained. "But my wife's been begging for a station wagon and finally I gave in. Man, I hated to part with the Pontiac. Just had it overhauled."

His curiosity aroused, my husband asked, "Are you talking about the four-door Pontiac Catalina on the Buick lot?"

"That's the one. Whoever buys that car will get one fine deal."

36

IMPOSSIBLE TO BELIEVE

Having worked successfully as a real-estate salesman in Glendale, California, Dow Coffman was totally unprepared for the sales slump that occurred in 1947. Commissions paychecks fell off. Sales were at a standstill. Though Dow and his wife, Mary, economized in every way they could, eventually even their savings account was depleted.

Bills—car payments, rent, and a host of other debts—remained unpaid. The Coffmans put on a good front. Not one of their many friends suspected their financial plight.

To further complicate matters, Mr. Coffman was forced to enter the hospital for an emergency appendix operation.

His mental anxiety hindered his recovery. In desperation he turned to the Bible for direction. When he read the Scripture admonition in James 5:14,15, he called the elders of his church to come and pray for him. After they had left, he pondered the words, ". . . and the prayer of faith shall save the sick man." *Hmmm,* Dow thought, *God cares for the whole man. He is as concerned about my debts, including my doctor and hospital bills, as I am.*

96/IT COULDN'T HAPPEN, BUT IT DID

In renewed dedication Dow whispered, "I believe! Take my debts, Lord, and do with them what you will."

A day or two later, a real-estate friend called to tell Mr. Coffman that one of his prospects had decided to buy a lot he had shown him weeks before. His friend told Dow he'd be happy to consummate the deal for him.

Two days passed. Another phone call. This time it was a woman who wanted to talk to Mr. Coffman.

"Mr. Coffman," she began. "You may not remember me, but you showed me an apartment house about a year ago. Is it still for sale?"

Cautiously Dow answered, "It is."

"I've decided to buy it."

While Mr. Coffman recovered at home, a buyer came to his house (not to the office) to confer with him. Months before, Dow had informed him of the availability of a $65,000 piece of income property. Within two days, with the help of the same real-estate friend, the deal was closed. All of the Coffman bills, including the tithe they owed their church, were paid.

"I can't believe it," Dow told Mary.

"Nor I," she answered. "But it's true."

37

VEIL OF SAFETY

It was 1942. Harvey and Ruth Widman were passengers on a freighter somewhere in mid-Atlantic, Congo bound. The ship, traveling in a complete blackout (even the faint glow from a sailor's cigarette was strictly forbidden), had broken away from a huge convoy. Now it was on its own. The trip so far had its moments of peril, none of them disastrous.

However, one night the captain and his crew discovered another ship, no doubt a German raider, in hot pursuit. They did everything they could to outrun and outwit the enemy. They zigzagged full speed ahead. Yet their pursuers steadily gained on them.

Ruth and Harvey felt much like the Israelites in the wilderness—"Lord, have you brought us this far, only to destroy us?"

Just when all hope had vanished, God answered that question by stirring up a rain squawl and dropping it like a thick veil between the two vessels.

Ship, crew, and passengers reached their destinations safely.

38

OF COURSE!

One day during the time when Julia Bengtson taught small children in a Christian elementary school, little Mike came to her, greatly distressed. Choking sobs, he showed her a small, lightweight glider from which a small piece of the tail had been broken.

"It's Jimmy's," he explained. "He let me play with it. And the wind grabbed it and bashed it against a tree. When I picked it up the tail was gone."

"Perhaps we can find it," Julia answered, hoping to comfort the boy.

"The piece is too small. I looked and looked. . . ." He hesitated. "Do you think God could help?"

"Of course! I'll round up the children while you ask him."

When Julia saw that the area they were to search was covered with small pebbles the same color as the glider, she lost hope.

Nevertheless, she asked the children to spread out and begin their search. She decided to scan the area where the accident occurred. She had taken only two or three steps when she saw it—a tiny piece from the glider tail, no larger than a dime.

The children cheered.

Walking back to their classroom with Mike, Julia asked, "Did you pray?"

"You better believe I did," he told her. "And God heard me, didn't He?"

39

PREDATED PRAYER

ANSWER

During the height of the Japanese-Chinese War, missionary Hjalmer Gravem worked in inland China. His wife, Helen, and their five children lived on the island of Cheung Chao off the coast of Hong Kong, where the American school for missionaries had been relocated from the mainland.

In 1941 the American consul ordered the American school moved to the States.

Helen did not want to leave the Orient without her husband, whose furlough was long overdue. Assessing the situation, she decided that, since the S.S. Pierce (on which she had been traveling) would stop at Shanghai, she would make arrangements to stay in the city until Hjalmer arrived—*provided* he made it through the war zone. "Lord, guide him and guard him," she prayed.

She soon learned that her plans were for naught. The ships's passengers were told they must remain on board because Shanghai bulged with refugees who had fled from battle territory. However, a pilot boat was permitted to bring messages from shore.

A surprise! A letter from Hjalmer! His message: He

and two women missionaries had managed to escape. They had arrived in Shanghai the previous day on bicycles. He would be permitted to come aboard the next morning and proceed with his family to America!

40

ORDERED BY THE LORD

It was February 1948. The Communist upheaval in China had led the American consul to urge the evacuation of all American missionaries. Only a few weeks earlier a doctor and two women missionaries had been murdered by Communist bandits because they refused to deny they were American citizens.

Heeding the consul's directive, Paul Backlund, five missonary comrades, and a Chinese family of five fled Kingchow, Hupeh, China. Since their escape route would take them through bandit territory they drove as rapidly as the bumpy roads allowed. They failed, however, to take into account any change in temperature.

By midafternoon the sun had thawed the muddy roadbeds and slowed the travelers to a crawl. Making matters worse, the smaller truck grounded and stalled repeatedly. Each delay cause increased anxiety.

Finally, after towing a smaller vehicle through an exceptionally muddy area onto a newer, firmer roadbed they relaxed. Now they would be able to travel at a faster pace, they reasoned.

Peace of mind soon dissipated, however. A truckload of Chinese soldiers sped toward them and motioned for them to stop. Waving their arms excitedly, they shouted, "Kung ch'an tang shao che tsu!" (The Communists are burning cars!")

"Where?"

"Ahead. About five kilometers."

Reluctantly the refugees turned and retraced their snail-paced muddy trek to a small village they had passed. There they would seek food and shelter for the night.

It wasn't until they were settled for the night that Missionary Backlund realized the significance of their forced retreat. If they hadn't been warned, they too would have suffered badly, perhaps fatally, at the hands of the truck-burning bandits.

41

FORETASTE OF HEAVEN

Lucille and Harold Gates of Phoenix, Arizona, know that God answers prayer. How quickly had never been an issue until Harold's mother, a sweet Christian woman who had lived with them for twenty-seven years, became seriously ill.

Since Harold suffered greatly from asthma attacks, he needed whatever rest he could get at night so that he could work by day. Consequently Lucille decided to sleep in the same room as his mother, who chattered deliriously most of the time.

Because the mother had to be watched constantly, Lucille slept little. One night, feeling that she had reached the limit of her strength, Lucille prayed, "Dear Lord, please calm Mother and give her peace so that both she and I can rest."

Almost immediately the room grew quiet. Her mother-in-law ceased tossing about. Then Lucille heard her speak softly, almost in a whisper: "Oh! It's beautiful . . . like snow . . . so white and clean." Later, "Look at all the flowers. How lovely they are." Then she relaxed, and both she and Lucille slept through the night.

Lucille's mother-in-law passed away shortly afterward. But in that interim her delirious restlessness never returned.

42

ONE THING LED TO ANOTHER

In one of his messages, later partially reiterated in his newsletter, the *Quarterly Yoke,* Dr. D. Elton Trueblood spoke of his and his wife's longing to meet the Christians behind the Iron Curtain.

He knew that his best chance for a fruitful visit to Russia would have to be arranged by the Baptist World Alliance.

One day, quite by chance, he met the Executive Director of the Baptist World Alliance on a plane. As a result of that chance meeting, he was asked to speak at the Executive Committee's meeting in Louisville in December 1974.

To his surprise and delight, four Russian Christians attended that meeting. Following his address to the group, Dr. Trueblood was introduced to the Russian representatives. He felt an immediate rapport with the men.

Some months later, on the basis of confidence established between the Russians and Dr. Trueblood in Louisville, he and his wife received an official invitation asking them to be June 1975 guests of the Union of Evangelical Christian Baptists in the U.S.S.R.

This invitation became the document that enabled

Dr. Trueblood and his wife to secure visas and to enter Russia without difficulty. When they arrived at the Moscow airport the presence of their hosts speeded their entrance to the extent that they were not asked to open thier suitcases.

In Russia they enjoyed what they believe was an extremely fruitful visit out of which came this appraisal by Dr. Trueblood of their hosts' Christian faith.

He says: "It is not a mild religion such as we observe in the West. A mild religion would be totally incapable of surviving in contemporary Russia. The only faith that is capable of survival is one that builds a very hot fire. Any other would go out and go out quickly."

43

A DREAM AND A STOLEN TRACTOR

When my father purchased a brand new tractor, the youngest children were delighted—not because of the time and labor it would save, but because of the rides they begged for and received.

One day shortly afterward, when we returned from a visit with relatives in a nearby town, Dad discovered that the tractor was gone. Dismayed, he exclaimed, "Someone must have stolen it!"

He spread the word to neighbors and friends. No one, it seemed, had any idea what had happened to the vehicle.

"I'll have to find a partner for Ned," he said, referring to the horse he had retired when he purchased the tractor. Buying a new tractor was out of the question.

Shortly afterward a friend (the man who had driven me to the doctor prior to my appendix operation) called. "Charles," he began excitedly, "I can tell you who stole your tractor."

"Who? How?" my father asked.

"I had a dream last night," his friend told him. "In my dream I saw a man from East Brittle Fork using your tractor to plow his field."

"What color was it?"

"Orange."

"But my tractor was red."

"It doesn't matter. The man must have repainted it. I know it's yours. Don't ask me how, I just know."

"All right, let's go and investigate."

Dad's friend was right. On close inspection they discovered that the tractor had been camouflaged with newly applied orange paint.

We never could understand why or how Dad's friend learned about the tractor in a dream. "It couldn't happen," Dad often commented, "but it did."

44

CHOICES: LIFE'S BUILDING BLOCKS

For want of a nail a shoe was lost; for want of a shoe a horse was lost; for want of a horse a rider was lost; for want of a rider a battle was lost; for want of a battle a war was lost. All for the want of a nail.

I've always thought this variation of George Herbert's maxim could as well have been expressed affirmatively. For example: Because of a nail the horse was shod that served the rider who fought the battle that won the war.

In every life there is a sequence of incidents that interact with each other to fashion the direction of life. Journalist/theologian Dr. Harold Lindsell speaks of such interaction when he describes his life.

In 1933 his health failed, and he went to a summer resort in the Catskill mountains to recuperate.

There, while contemplating going to college, another guest asked, "Have you ever thought of going to Wheaton College?" Lindsell had never heard of the college. He decided to write for the college catalog.

When he learned that smoking, dancing, movies, and card playing were forbidden (though he didn't object to any of these activities), he decided this was the place for him to pursue college work seriously.

What else was there to do? He applied for admittance and was accepted.

At Wheaton the 1936 revival transformed his life. And during his stay at Wheaton he met Dr. McQuilkin, Billy and Ruth Graham, and Mrs. Graham's father, Dr. L. Nelson Bell. It was through his association with Dr. McQuilkin that he learned about Columbia Bible College, a school where he taught following graduate studies.

At Columbia he met Marian Bolinder, the girl he married. "If I hadn't gone to Wheaton," he says, "I wouldn't have gone to Columbia. If I hadn't gone to Columbia I wouldn't have met the woman I married."

Later, recommended by Carl F. H. Henry, he moved to the Northern Bible Seminary. Again, his association with Dr. Henry led to their becoming founding faculty members at Fuller Theological Seminary.

In 1964, through the influence of Dr. Henry and Dr. L. Nelson Bell, he became a member of *Christianity Today's* editorial family.

All these things happened, Dr. Lindsell claims, "because God led me to Wheaton College. A day-by-day miracle, I call it. This decision brought me to the Bible, which has become the polestar of my life and has opened countless doors of opportunity for service in the name of the Master whom I have come to love and to serve with abandonment."

45

AN UNSCHEDULED CALL

One day as Melva Wickman, a well-known Bible teacher, walked down a street in Seattle, Washington, she felt a strange concern for a man who shunned the church and all it stood for. It was as if a voice said, "Go visit him."

That hard, bitter, cruel man? Melva thought. No way!

The voice persisted.

Eventually Melva succumbed to its directive. She turned on her heel and headed for the street where the man, a big burly individual, lived. She found him tending his garden.

"Hi!" she greeted in as cheerful a voice as she could muster.

The man put down his spade. "Mrs. Wickman! What are you doing here?" he asked.

"I honestly don't know," Melva answered. "I just felt God wanted me to come. Is there anything I can do for you?"

The man bit his lip; his eyes brimmed with tears. "Yes, there is," he stammered. "You can pray for me. I need God."

46

BUTTON, BUTTON, WHERE IS MY BUTTON?

It was mid-November, with snow falling, when Hugh McLeod drove his wife, Ceil, to the ambulance entrance at St. Luke's hospital in Fargo, North Dakota, following an attack of back pain. He helped her into a wheelchair, then rushed back to get her suitcase and to move his car to the hospital parking lot.

Fifteen minutes later, when Ceil had been eased into bed and hooked up to traction, she saw Hugh glance at his gold sport jacket, and she noted that a button was missing. It was an expensive button, with embossed leaping horses etched on bronze. It was impossible to match. Ceil watched Hugh finger the empty buttonhole.

"When did you lose your button?" she asked.

"I don't know. I remember buttoning it at home in all that rush. Shucks, I'll never be able to match it. I'll have to buy a whole new set."

Ceil expressed her sympathy.

"Don't worry about it," Hugh answered, "After all, it's only a button...." He stopped suddenly, obsessed with a new thought. "Hey, why don't we ask God to find the button? But first let's ask Him to ease your pain."

Twenty minutes later the phone rang. Ceil picked up the receiver. It was Hugh, his voice buoyant. "You'll never believe it, Honey. There was a bare spot where the ambulance had parked just a few feet from our car. There lay the button, undamaged! I'd never have found it had it fallen an inch away in the snow. I guess God knows as much about buttons as He does lilies of the field."

47

HIS DREAM—A HIDDEN DOOR OF HOPE

When World War Two broke out, Norman Rohrer, age fourteen, quit school to help his father on the family farm. In 1949 he was still on the farm. He had dreamed that someday he might become a writer, but without a high school diploma the future looked bleak.

As the bass in a Youth for Christ quartet planning a trip to Montrose, Pennsylvania, to sing at a Bible conference, one day Norm told his mother he might hitchhike to New York City to see the sights before he returned home. He said *might* because he had other plans.

The morning the quartet was ready to leave Montrose, Norm pretended he was asleep until the other quartet members went to eat breakfast. The moment they left, Norm leaped from his bed and threw some of his clothes in his trombone case. Then, after writing a note asking the quartet tenor to take his suitcase home, he fled.

In midtown on a cross-country road, he signaled his need for a ride. The driver of a Cadillac heading west picked him up. Each succeeding ride took him farther and farther from his home. Eventually he reached Cleveland, Ohio.

As he pondered his future in a YMCA room that night he wept. Yet he felt compelled to continue his trek. He asked God to direct his future. Perhaps, he thought, he could make his way to Alaska. He'd heard that salaries were high in the far North.

The next day a truckdriver let Norm out at a small town—Wheaton, Illinois. He asked a woman tending her flowers about a place to stay for the night.

"We don't have any motels," she told him. "But since it is July, you can probably rent a room at the Wheaton College dorm. I've heard they only charge fifty cents a night."

When Norman paid for his room the next morning, Dr. Authur Volle asked, "Do you expect to enroll in Wheaton College?"

Norm shook his head, explaining his lack of qualifications. "I thought I might try to make it to Alaska."

"Would you like to go to college?"

Like to go to college? Norm's eyes saucered. "Of course, but . . . ."

"I'll see what I can do," the man told him.

At the Admissions Office he arranged for a batch of psychological tests that qualified Norm to go to Elmhurst to take the five two-hour GED tests developed for the Armed Forces. At the end of the week he paid the $4.38 cost and walked out of the building with a high-school diploma!

Four years later he was graduated from Wheaton College.

Was his early dream fulfilled?

Indeed! Who but author/editor/instructor Norman Roher is as well-known in the evangelical publishing field?

48

HER TORCH OF FREEDOM

"At the root of every nervous disorder lies an unsurrendered self, the ego."

Frances Schneider gasped. Though her mental distress had plummeted to a new low, she couldn't believe the words of the radio broadcast. She, a clergyman's wife, *unsurrendered,* with an ego god robbing her of peace and joy? Unthinkable?

But as the weeks and months dragged by, she came to believe that the message was true. Panic-stricken by day and wakeful by night, life grew unbearable. Normal activities became unconquerable monsters; every automobile ride became a potential accident. World problems assumed personal identity; each hungry child became her own responsibility. Meanwhile the radio message repeated itself over and over in her mind, haunting every waking hour. One day while doing the family ironing she rebelled. Angry, she shouted, "I'm tired of this self-examination. It's like a dark tunnel that has no end. I want out. I want peace and power and light!"

Suddenly, as if directed by an unseen power, she walked to her desk and picked up a pen and a sheet of paper. At the top of the page she wrote in big letters: MY SINS AND MY FEARS. Then she divided the page into two columns. One she titled "The Past," the other "The Present."

Slowly, deliberately, she listed past and present fears and sins. She sighed deeply as she laid down her pen. Somehow the exercise had been therapeutic. She relaxed for the first time in days.

A new inspiration! She retrieved her pen. With strong, firm hand, diagonally across the page, she wrote: "And all that I can't recall."

Then she took a match from a kitchen cupboard and walked to the outdoor fireplace. Reverently she knelt, struck the match, and lit the paper.

As the flame consumed it she repeated Philippians 4:6-7: "Have no anxiety about anything, but in everything by prayer and supplication with thanksgiving let your rquests be known to God. And the peace of God, which passes all understanding, will keep your hearts and your minds in Christ Jesus" (RSV).

With thanksgiving? Yes! She prayed, "Thank you, Lord."

A meadowlark, full-throated and free, broke the ensuing stillness. "I am free!" Frances cried.

As she recalls this experience she says, "At that moment the peace of God that passes all understanding filled my heart and life with light and power. Like the lark on wing, I *was* free."

49

DESERT VENTURE

Native Californians Randy and Charlene Swanson had been married three years when they decided they had accumulated sufficient funds to take a year off and travel extensively.

After they had mapped out what their parents called an incredible itinerary, they arranged for necessary medical shots, passports, and visas.

Traveling in a Volkswagen camper, they drove through California, Arizona, Mexico, and Central and Southern America to the tip of Chile's toe. Then they turned northward to Rio de Janeiro.

From Rio they flew to Portugal and ferried the camper to Morocco. Then began the trek through Africa to Cape Town and north again.

For some reason the Sahara Desert presented a challenge. "Let's drive across it," Randy suggested.

"Alone? Isn't that dangerous?" Charlene countered.

"I guess so. But if we carry sufficient supplies and take it easy we ought to make it. Others have."

So began a long hot trek over roadways that, for the most part, were deeply corrugated. Up! Down! Up! Down! They felt like pawns in the hands of a giant juggler. Frequently they castigated themselves for their folly. But they persisted.

One day close to the noon hour, on a section of road with extremely deep grooves, they heard what sounded like an explosion. The Volkswagen stalled. Investigating, Randy discovered that the left front and left rear shock absorber mounts had broken.

Stupid people, he thought. What on earth will we do? Miles from nowhere . . . automobile parts inaccessible . . . mechanics nonexistent!

As he and Charlene assessed their problem they recalled the abandoned cars and bleached bones they had passed. Would that be their fate?

They prayed—how they prayed! God was their only hope.

When the sun became unbearable, they dug a shallow protective trench under the car and crawled into its shelter. The ensuing minutes seemed like hours. Then, suddenly, they heard the sound of a truck in the distance.

The driver shook his bushy head when he learned the young couple's plight.

"You need a welding job," he said.

"Welding job?" Randy challenged. "Here in the desert?"

The man chuckled. "Strangest thing—I'm delivering an acetylene welding torch to a fellow in the next town. Got it in my truck. But I don't know how to use it."

Neither did Randy, but he was game to try. Once

he had watched his dad use one. But he'd need a welding rod. Would a clothes hanger do?

It would.

Eventually, exhausted and sweaty, yet highly elated, Randy and his benefactor completed the suspension repair.

With a hearty "thank you" and a warm "God bless you" Randy and Charlene bade their new friend goodbye.

It couldn't happen, but it did. Randy and Charlene finished their trek and drove hundreds of miles in the States, the front and rear suspension still intact!

50

HOW COULD IT HAPPEN?

I was driving alone in Phoenix one Monday afternoon, intent on getting home to greet out-of-state visitors.

En route my thoughts turned to the ill fortune that had befallen a friend who lived in a nursing home that I was passing. Injured in an industrial accident, Dave was paralyzed from the neck down.

I passed the nursing home, grateful that my husband and I had visited Dave a few days previously.

Suddenly I felt a strange compulsion to turn back and visit him again. But I need to get home, I told myself.

The compulsion persisted.

I turned the car around and drove back to the nursing home. The moment I entered Dave's room I sensed that something was terribly wrong. Beads of perspiration trickled down his forehead. I reached for his hand.

"Dave, you're ice cold!"

"Call a nurse, *quick*," he cried.

I did.

"I'll take over," she told me.

Later I learned that, because attendants had failed to check his catheter, urine had backed up in his system—a condition which, if not remedied at once, could cause sudden death.

Whenever I reflect on this incident, I recall miraculous time-meshing experiences other people have had.

* * *

Asked to dispose of some of the flowers used to decorate their church during its seventy-fifth anniversary, Charlotte Springer and her husband decided to deliver a lovely chrysanthemum plant to one of the elderly couples who had not been able to attend the festivities.

Since the hour was late and their two children restless, Mr. Springer said, "Let's get the kids to bed. I'll deliver the plant first thing in the morning."

Charlotte shook her head. "I feel we ought to stop with it now."

"Okay, if you insist."

When they arrived at the couple's home no one responded to the doorbell. They tried the door. It was locked. They contacted a neighbor with whom they knew a daughter had left a key.

Once in the home, the Springers found the woman lying on the floor, her husband bending over trying to help her get up. She'd suffered a stroke only moments before the Springers arrived.

* * *

When Bob Page's mother died he drove two hun-

IT COULDN'T HAPPEN, BUT IT DID/127

dred miles from San Jose, California, to Tulare to make arrangements for her funeral. Because he knew she wanted to be buried close to her husband, who had died thirty years previously, he inquired about cemetery lots in that area. None were available. They had been sold out for fifteen years.

Disappointed, he made other arrangements.

The next day, a few hours prior to his mother's memorial service, the funeral director called. "You won't believe this," he said, "but a man who owned a cemetery lot just a few feet from your father's sold the lot to the cemetery today. I'll make arrangements for an exchange. Okay?"

* * *

I could go on endlessly. My files are full of such experiences. A missionary or a student receives funds at a precise moment of need. A mother or father feels constrained to pray for a child who, they learn later, faced danger at the time they prayed.

What do these experiences mean?

That, ordinarily they cannot happen, yet in God's mysterious providence, they do!